BURNING
AS LIGHT

THIRTY-SEVEN POEMS BY

Andrew Young

WITH WOOD-ENGRAVINGS BY
JOAN HASSALL

CHOSEN BY
LEONARD CLARK

RUPERT HART-DAVIS
LONDON
1967

Published in Great Britain by
Rupert Hart-Davis Ltd
3 Upper James Street Golden Square London W.1.

B67-21995

Printed by Compton Printing Ltd
London and Aylesbury

Contents

THE OLD TREE   5

THE DEAD BIRD   6

THE SHADOW   6

ROTHER IN FLOOD   7

IN MOONLIGHT   8

THE EVENING STAR   9

THE BEECH   10

THE DEAD CRAB   11

THE SUNBEAMS   12

THE SHEAF   13

THE MEN   14

A WINDY DAY   15

THE STOCKDOVES   16

THE SWANS   17

IN DECEMBER   17

THISTLEDOWN   18

LAST SNOW   18

THE FEAR   19

REFLECTIONS ON THE RIVER   20

MIST   21

THE EAGLE   22

THE WHITE BLACKBIRD   22

THE CHALK CLIFF   23

MAY FROST   24

JULY   24

SNOW HARVEST   25

AFTER THE GALE   25

SNOW   26

SOUTH DOWNS   27

THE MISSEL-THRUSH   27

THE FROGS   28

A PREHISTORIC CAMP   28

THE FLESH SCRAPER   29

ON THE COMMON   29

WALKING ON THE CLIFF   30

THE CUCKOO   31

Extract from NICODEMUS   32

The Old Tree

The wood shakes in the breeze
  Lifting its antlered heads;
Green leaf nor brown one sees
  But the rain's glassy beads.

One tree-trunk in the wood
  No tangled head uprears,
A stump of soft touchwood
  Dead to all hopes and fears.

Even the round-faced owl
  That shakes out his long hooting
With the moon cheek-a-jowl
  Could claw there no safe footing.

Riddled by worms' small shot,
  Empty of all desire,
It smoulders in its rot,
  A pillar of damp fire.

The Dead Bird

Ah, that was but the wind
Your soft down stirred,
O bird, lying with sidelong head;
These open eyes are blind,
I cannot frighten you away;
You are so very dead
I almost say
'You are not a dead *bird*.'

The Shadow

Dark ghost
That from tree-trunk to tree-trunk tost,
Flows with me still,
When on the shoulder of the hill
The late sunrise
Tangles its rainbows on my eyes —

Although
Each time I wave to you below
I see you stand
And wave back with a distant hand,
I ask, Can you be mine,
O shade gigantic and divine?

Rother in Flood

Between twin banks the Rother
  With slow contentment goes;
Bush-sprinkled lakes spread this side and
    the other
  Flowing as the wind flows.

High on the upper lands
  White-cowled oasthouses stare
And piled poles in hop gardens seem like
    hands
  Whose fingers point in prayer.

Gathered by stormy weather
  The rooks and sea-gulls meet
Like black angels and white mingling
    together
  At God's last judgement-seat.

In Moonlight

We sat where boughs waved on the ground
But made no sound;
'They cannot shake me off,'
Shrieked the black dwarf,
Impudent elf,
That was the shadow of myself.

I said to him, 'We must go now';
But from his bough
He laughed, securely perched,
'Then you rise first;'
It seemed to me
He spoke in wicked courtesy.

We rose and 'Take my hand,' he whined,
Though like the wind
Each waving bough he leapt;
And as we stept
Down the steep track
He seemed to grow more hunched and black.

The Evening Star

I saw a star shine in bare trees
That stood in their dark effigies;
With voice so clear and close it sang
That like a bird it seemed to hang
Rising and falling with the wind,
Twigs on its rosy breast outlined.

An obvious moon high on the night
And haloed by a rainbow light
Sounded as loud as silver bell
And trees in flight before it fell,
Their shadows straggling on the road
Where glacier of soft moonlight flowed.

But moon nor star-untidy sky
Could catch my eye as that star's eye;
For still I looked on that same star,
That fitful, fiery Lucifer,
Watching with mind as quiet as moss
Its light nailed to a burning cross.

The Beech

Strength leaves the hand I lay on this beech-bole
   So great-girthed, old and high;
Its sprawling arms like iron serpents roll
   Between me and the sky.

One elbow on the sloping earth it leans,
   That steeply falls beneath,
As though resting a century it means
   To take a moment's breath.

Its long thin buds in glistering varnish dipt
   Are swinging up and down
While one young beech that winter left unstript
   Still wears its withered crown.

At least gust of the wind the great tree heaves
   From heavy twigs to groin;
The wind sighs as it rakes among dead leaves
   For some lost key or coin.

And my blood shivers as away it sweeps
   Rustling the leaves that cling
Too late to that young withered beech that keeps
   Its autumn in the spring.

The Dead Crab

A rosy shield upon its back,
That not the hardest storm could crack,
From whose sharp edge projected out
Black pin-point eyes staring about;
Beneath, the well-knit cote-armure
That gave to its weak belly power;
The clustered legs with plated joints
That ended in stiletto points;
The claws like mouths it held outside:
I cannot think this creature died
By storm or fish or sea-fowl harmed
Walking the sea so heavily armed;
Or does it make for death to be
Oneself a living armoury?

The Sunbeams

The tired road climbed the hill
Through trees with light-spots never still,
Gold mouths that drew apart and singled
And ran again and met and mingled,
Two, three or five or seven,
No other way than souls that love in heaven.

Sunny and swift and cool
They danced there like Bethesda's pool;
Ah, if in those pale kissing suns
My halting feet could bathe but once
No slender stick would crack,
My footstep falling on its brittle back.

The Sheaf

I'd often seen before
That sheaf of corn hung from the bough —
Strange in a wood a sheaf of corn
Though by the winds half torn
And thrashed by rain to empty straw.
And then to-day I saw
A small pink twitching snout
And eyes like black beads sewn in fur
Peep from a hole in doubt,
And heard on dry leaves go tat-tat
The stiff tail of the other rat.
And now as the short day grows dim
And here and there farms in the dark
Turn to a spark,
I on my stumbling way think how
With indistinguishable limb
And tight tail round each other's head
They'll make to-night one ball in bed,
Those long-tailed lovers who have come
To share the pheasants' harvest-home.

The Men

I sat to listen to each sound
Of leaf on twig or ground
And finch that cracked a seed
Torn from a limp and tarnished weed
And rapid flirt of wings
As bluetits flew and used as swings
The bines of old man's beard,
When suddenly I heard
Those men come crashing through the wood
And voices as they stood,
And dog that yelped and whined
At each shrill scent his nose could find;
And knowing that it meant small good
To some of us who owned that wood,
Badger, stoat, rabbit, rook and jay
And smoky dove that clattered away,
Although no ill to me at least,
I too crept off like any stealthy beast.

A Windy Day

This wind brings all dead things to life,
Branches that lash the air like whips
And dead leaves rolling in a hurry
Or peering in a rabbits' bury
Or trying to push down a tree;
Gates that fly open to the wind
And close again behind,
And fields that are a flowing sea
And make the cattle look like ships;

Straws glistening and stiff
Lying on air as on a shelf
And pond that leaps to leave itself;
And feathers too that rise and float,
Each feather changed into a bird,
And line-hung sheets that crack and strain;
Even the sun-greened coat,
That through so many winds has served,
The scarecrow struggles to put on again.

The Stockdoves

They rose up in a twinkling cloud
And wheeled about and bowed
To settle on the trees
Perching like small clay images.

Then with a noise of sudden rain
They clattered off again
And over Ballard Down
They circled like a flying town.

Though one could sooner blast a rock
Than scatter that dense flock
That through the winter weather
Some iron rule has held together.

Yet in another month from now
Love like a spark will blow
Those birds the country over
To drop in trees, lover by lover.

The Swans

How lovely are these swans,
That float like high proud galleons
Cool in the summer heat,
And waving leaf-like feet
Divide with narrow breasts of snow
In a smooth surge
This water that is mostly sky;
So lovely that I know
Death cannot kill such birds,
It could but wound them, mortally.

In December

I watch the dung-cart stumble by
　Leading the harvest to the fields,
That from cow-byre and stall and sty
　The farmstead in the winter yields.

Like shocks in a reaped field of rye
　The small black heaps of lively dung
Sprinkled in the grass-meadow lie
　Licking the air with smoky tongue.

This is Earth's food that man piles up
　And with his fork will thrust on her,
And Earth will lie and slowly sup
　With her moist mouth through half the year.

Thistledown

Silver against blue sky
These ghosts of day float by,
Fitful, irregular,
Each one a silk-haired star,
Till from the wind's aid freed
They settle on their seed.

Not by the famished light
Of a moon-ridden night
But by clear sunny hours
Gaily these ghosts of flowers
With rise and swirl and fall
Dance to their burial.

Last Snow

Although the snow still lingers
Heaped on the ivy's blunt webbed fingers
And painting tree-trunks on one side,
Here in this sunlit ride
The fresh unchristened things appear,
Leaf, spathe and stem,
With crumbs of earth clinging to them
To show the way they came
But no flower yet to tell their name,
And one green spear
Stabbing a dead leaf from below
Kills winter at a blow.

The Fear

How often I turn round
To face the beast that bound by bound
Leaps on me from behind,
Only to see a bough that heaves
With sudden gust of wind
Or blackbird raking withered leaves.

A dog may find me out
Or badger toss a white-lined snout;
And one day as I softly trod
Looking for nothing stranger than
A fox or stoat I met a man
And even that seemed not too odd.

And yet in any place I go
I watch and listen as all creatures do
For what I cannot see or hear,
For something warns me everywhere
That even in my land of birth
I trespass on the earth.

Reflections on the River

Rose-petals fall without a touch
As though it were too much
I should be standing by,
And poplars in no wind at all
Keep swaying left and right
With the slow motion of their height
Beneath a small white cloud that soon
Will pluck light from the dark and be the moon.

But where roach rise and bite the Ouse
Round ripples spread out like the first
Drops of a storm about to burst
And in the water toss the boughs
And crack the garden wall;
And as I gaze down in the sky
I see the whole vault shake
As though the heavens were seized with an earthquake.

Mist

Rain, do not fall
Nor rob this mist at all,
That is my only cell and abbey wall.

Wind, wait to blow
And let the thick mist grow,
That fills the rose-cup with a whiter glow.

Mist, deepen still
And the low valley fill;
You hide but taller trees, a higher hill.

Still, mist, draw close;
These gain by what they lose,
The taller trees and hill, the whiter rose.

All else begone,
And leave me here alone
To tread this mist where earth and sky are one.

The Eagle

He hangs between his wings outspread
   Level and still
And bends a narrow golden head,
   Scanning the ground to kill.

Yet as he sails and smoothly swings
   Round the hill-side,
He looks as though from his own wings
   He hung down crucified.

The White Blackbird

Gulls that in meadows stand,
The sea their native land,
Are not so white as you
Flitting from bough to bough,
You who are white as sin
To your black kith and kin.

The Chalk-Cliff

Blasted and bored and undermined
  By quarrying seas
Reared the erect chalk-cliff with black flints lined.
  (Flints drop like nuts from trees
When the frost bites
The chalk on winter nights.)

Save for frail shade of jackdaw's flight
  No night was there,
But blue-skyed summer and a cliff so white
  It stood like frozen air;
Foot slipped on damp
Chalk where the limpets camp.

With only purple of sea-stock
  And jackdaw's shade
To mitigate that blazing height of chalk
  I stood like a soul strayed
In paradise
Hiding my blinded eyes.

May Frost

It was the night May robbed September
Killing with frost the apple-bloom,
The sunset sunk to its last ember,
I climbed the dew-webbed combe;
There floating from the earth's round rim
I saw the red sun rise.
At first I only thought 'How soon,'
And then 'Surely I must be dying;
These are death's cobwebs on my eyes
That make the dawn so dim;'
And yet my sight was lying:
The frost had set on fire the full-faced moon.

July

Darker the track to-day
Than any cloudy March or April day
     When nesting birds sang louder,
For hazels hazels, elders elders meet,
Tangle and trip the sun's pale dancing feet
     That beat it to white powder.

That day in January,
I climbed the hill to this wood's sanctuary,
     The track was plain enough;
Now bryony crowds its stars yellow as honey
And close against my face hemp-agrimony
     Pushes its purple faces.

But I may find again
When autumn's fires sink under winter's rain
     A clearer way to pass,
As when that sun with a wan ray of hope
Striking a hollow on the frost furred slope
     Wet one green patch of grass.

Snow Harvest

The moon that now and then last night
Glanced between clouds in flight
Saw the white harvest that spread over
The stubble fields and even roots and clover.

It climbed the hedges, overflowed
And trespassed on the road,
Weighed down fruit-trees and when winds woke
From white-thatched roofs rose in a silver smoke.

How busy is the world to-day!
Sun reaps, rills bear away
The lovely harvest of the snow
While bushes weep loud tears to see it go.

After the Gale

I pity trees that all their life
Have ivy for a wife
Or with dark mistletoe they bear
Keep Christmas through the year.

So seeing oak-twigs grow on thorn
Where they were never born,
And sprays of ash-keys and pine-cones
Grow on a briar at once.

I blamed the gale that through the night
Had with perverse delight
Quartered rich children on the poor
Like foundlings at their door.

Snow

Ridged thickly on black bough
    And foaming on twig-fork in swollen lumps
At flirt of bird-wing or wind's sough
    Plump snow tumbled on snow softly with sudden dumps.

Where early steps had made
    A wavering track through the white-blotted road
Breaking its brightness with blue shade,
    Snow creaked beneath my feet with snow heavily shod.

I reached a snow-thatched rick
    Where men sawed bedding off for horse and cow;
There varnished straws were lying thick
    Paving with streaky gold the trodden silver snow.

Such light filled me with awe
    And nothing marred my paradisal thought,
That robin least of all I saw
    Lying too fast asleep, his song choked in his throat.

South Downs

No water cries among these hills,
   The mist hides and enlarges,
Though rain in every road-rut spills
   Where leaves have sunk their barges.

No freshet in a hollow brake
   Utters its shy cold fears,
Only the chiming sheep-bells make
   One Sabbath of the years.

The Missel-Thrush

That missel-thrush
Scorns to alight on a low bush,
And as he flies
And tree-top after tree-top tries,
His shadow flits
And harmlessly on tree-trunk hits.

Shutting his wings
He sways and sings and sways and sings,
And from his bough
As in deep water he looks through
He sees me there
Crawl at the bottom of the air.

The Frogs

Each night that I come down the strath
Frogs turn heels-over-head,
And their white bellies on the path
Tell where to tread.

Of fox with brush above the brake
And kestrel pinned to air
And thin dark river of a snake
Let them beware!

Fat acrobats, I watch them turn
Kicking the evening dew,
Till in white waves that ride the burn
I see frogs too.

A Prehistoric Camp

It was the time of year
   Pale lambs leap with thick leggings on
Over small hills that are not there,
   That I climbed Eggardon.

The hedgerows still were bare,
   None ever knew so late a year;
Birds built their nests in the open air,
   Love conquering their fear.

But there on the hill-crest,
   Where only larks or stars look down,
Earthworks exposed a vaster nest,
   Its race of men long flown.

The Flesh-Scraper

If I had sight enough
Might I not find a finger-print
Left on this flint
By Neolithic man or Kelt?
So knapped to scrape a wild beast's pelt,
The thumb below, fingers above,
See, my hand fits it like a glove.

On the Common

The chaffy seeds by the wind blown
Are here so strangely sown,
That one might almost say
The spider's-webs the bushes wear
Have been put down to hay,
And though no crop they bear
Ploughed and cross-ploughed on empty air,
So thick these hay-fields swarm,
That every gorse-bush is become a farm.

Walking on the Cliff

But for a sleepy gull that yawned
   And spread its wings and dropping disappeared
This evening would have dawned
   To the eternity my flesh has feared.

For too intent on a blackcap
   Perched like a miser on the yellow furze
High over Birling Gap,
   That sang 'Gold is a blessing not a curse,'

How near I was to stepping over
   The brink where the gull dropped to soar beneath.
While now safe as a lover
   I walk the cliff-edge arm in arm with Death.

The Cuckoo

This year the leaves were late and thin,
And my eye wandering softly in
Saw perched upon a topmost twig,
Small bird to have a voice so big,
A cuckoo with long tail behind,
Twig and bird aswing on the wind,
That rose and flew with outspread tail
Guiding his flight like steering sail.

I waited, listened; came again
Across the distance of the rain
'Cuckoo' so faint and far-away
It sounded out of yesterday,
Making me start with sudden fear
Lest spring that had seemed new and near
Was gone already. A sparrow hopped
In white plum-tree and blossom dropped.

Extract from

NICODEMUS

A Mystery

JOHN Nicodemus!
NICODEMUS My name! Who speaks the name I had forgotten?
My eyes are stupid coming from the light.
John, is it you? Have you been waiting here:
Still waiting? O how long ago it is
Since you and I stood talking at this door.
It was another life. I did not know
Your Master then; O John, I know Him now.
I had a mother once and she is dead;
I think she did not bear me till this hour.
Or 'born again' was what the Master said;
Have I been born again? O God, I pray
I be not cast out like a stillborn child.
He is to blame to let me go — But no;
I cannot now go back: never again.
It was a stillborn child my mother bore,
But I am come alive to-night. O John,

Not only I am born again to-night,
The world is born again. Look at the stars;
Though small they jostle in the sky for room,
Shining so bright, they drop down through the air;
Are they not born again? Look at the street;
The stones are nestling down to their hard sleep,
Stone nudging neighbour stone, whispering 'Friend,
Are we not born to-night?' Look at the door,
An open sepulchre; I went in dead,
Now I come out again and walk in heaven.
Who could have thought that our poor earth was heaven?
I kiss you, John, my brother.